The Battle of Britain

July to October 1940

Classic, Rare and Unseen Photographs
from the

Daily Mail

The Battle of Britain

July to October 1940

James Alexander

Trans
Atlantic
Press

Published by Transatlantic Press in 2010

Transatlantic Press
38 Copthorne Road
Croxley Green
Hertfordshire, WD3 4AQ, UK

Photographs © *Daily Mail Archive*
© Transatlantic Press 2010

A catalogue record for this book is available
from the British Library.

ISBN 978–1–907176–21–0
Printed in China

'Their finest hour'

The Battle of Britain raged from June to October 1940, a short but concentrated conflict which, had the outcome been different, might have seen a successful invasion by Germany, and a Nazi regime ruling Britain. The road to this brief but intense battle began when the appeasement policy of Neville Chamberlain's government towards the aggression of the Hitler regime finally failed in September 1939 with the German invasion of Poland, prompting Britain and France to declare war on Germany.

By the time Winston Churchill stepped into the position of Prime Minister on 10 May 1940, Germany had occupied Norway and Denmark, invaded the Netherlands and was well on the way to turning back the British Expeditionary Force in France; soon it would bring France to submission. The gravity of the British situation was brought home in the incredible rescue, 'Operation Dynamo', of over 330,000 Allied troops in the evacuation from Dunkirk during the nine days from 26 May to 4 June.

The success of this operation camouflaged the real losses to the British Army and the Royal Air Force in France, but the resolve of Fighter Command's Air Chief Marshal Hugh Dowding ensured that Britain retained a reserve of fighter aircraft, even though the Hurricane squadrons in France lost 200 machines – a significant proportion of the RAF total fighter strength. At this low point in Britain's fortunes, Churchill electrified and boosted the nation with his speech to the Commons on 4 June: 'We shall defend our island, whatever the cost may be. We shall fight on the beaches, we shall fight on the landing grounds, we shall fight in the fields and in the streets, we shall fight in the hills; we shall never surrender.'

Hitler and his Blitzkrieg commanders were understandably confident about their war machine but Nazi hubris bred false assumptions that would lead to Germany's unexpected defeat in the Battle of Britain. The Luftwaffe had dominated the skies of Western Europe during the Blitzkrieg; its task now was to crush the RAF and disable its aircraft production. Field Marshal Hermann Goering, the Luftwaffe commander, boasted that the RAF would be broken in four days and its production capability wiped out in four weeks. However, the RAF were not to succumb to Goering's plan. The Battle of Britain was to have four clear phases and on 18 June, Churchill predicted Britain's struggle for survival with his famous 'Finest Hour' speech.

The first phase of the German offensive, dubbed 'Kanalkampf' (translated 'Channel battles'), targeted Britain's shipping and coastal defences to bring home the country's vulnerability, isolation and dependence on sea transport. Traditional shipping routes made extensive use of the English Channel and the North Sea, placing convoys of ships within striking distance of German fighters and bombers, as well as heavy coastal guns sited close by in France. Early in this phase of the Battle, Britain's Radio Direction Finding (RDF) Chain (a prototype radar developed as an early warning system in the 1930s), proved effective in anticipating Luftwaffe raids, scrambling the fighter squadrons of Coastal Command to meet the Luftwaffe before they reached their targets. However, the German raiders employed teasing tactics, feinting raids to spook RAF aircraft into the air, calculating their flying time and the need to return to base to refuel. These same tactics kept the civilian population on constant alert, fearful that an air raid was imminent.

On 12 August, the pace and spread of German attacks stepped up as Goering set in motion preparations for a September invasion of the British Isles, code-named 'Operation Sealion'. This phase of the Battle was called 'Adlerangriff' or 'Eagle Attack' and was launched with massed attacks by hundreds of bombers and fighters on 13 August, 'Adlertag' ('Eagle Day'). By mid-August, fine weather meant the Luftwaffe had clear skies for their daylight raids and a series of attacks were raised on Britain's RDF Chain with the intention of permanently disabling it. The speed with which the RDF was restored caused the Luftwaffe to draw incorrect conclusions about the robustness of the system; if they had persevered with their plan, Britain would have been much more vulnerable. In fact the Luftwaffe failed to destroy the RAF's fleet on the ground and although the Messerschmitt Bf109 was superior to the RAF's main defensive aircraft, the Hurricane and its glamorous cousin the Supermarine Spitfire, the Luftwaffe was unable to get the better of Fighter Command in the air, paying a heavy price in machines and pilots. The 15 August brought serious losses to the Luftwaffe – they named it 'Black Thursday'; on 18 August – 'the Hardest Day' – losses on both sides were equally high.

The next phase of the Battle, which began on 24 August, concentrated on the destruction of RAF airfields. Although the Luftwaffe killed many ground personnel and damaged airfields with monotonous regularity, they still did not succeed in destroying Fighter Command's defensive capability. Much of this failure must be attributed to the tactical skills of Fighter Command who had to calculate their response to German raids with the greatest care: scrambling squadrons too soon might lead to their running out of fuel just as German raiders were approaching their targets. Luftwaffe Command knew that RDF would alert Fighter Command and often set traps for the hard-pressed RAF, which quickly realised the cat-and-mouse element to German attacks and that responding too soon or too late or with too few or too many aircraft could have disastrous results. Dowding's conservative approach, emulated by Air Vice Marshal Keith Park, in charge of 11 Group, kept up a continuous response to Luftwaffe attack, despite the exhaustion of pilots and the loss of aircraft.

At the beginning of September 1940, RAF Fighter Command was at breaking point: the RAF had lost 300 pilots in August alone, and had only been able to replace 260 of them; in the 14 days leading up to 4 September, 295 RAF fighters were destroyed, with 171 badly damaged; and in 11 Group, which bore the brunt of Luftwaffe raids, 6 out of 7 sector stations were almost out of action. Nevertheless, despite being on the brink of collapse, Fighter Command had succeeded in convincing the Luftwaffe that its strategy to destroy British fighter capability had failed. Alongside this state of affairs, in late August, German bombers had dropped bombs on civilians in

London; in response, Bomber Command launched a night raid on Berlin on 25 August. Inexplicably, this enraged Hitler, who had given strict instructions that the Luftwaffe should not bomb civilian targets unless he specifically ordered it, and led to a change in the German's line of attack when, on 4 September, his response was the escalated bombing of British cities. Just at the point where Fighter Command was on its knees with a shortage of planes and pilots, as well as its airfields being at breaking point, the Luftwaffe halted their effective strategy for a change in tactics.

On 7 September, the new German approach ushered in the fourth and final phase of the Battle of Britain with the beginning of the Blitz, as 950 German aircraft attacked London in the first and last massed daylight raid on the capital; 300 civilians were killed and 1,300 seriously wounded. For the next 57 consecutive days, London was remorselessly bombed in night raids. Fighter Command was amazed at this development, which perversely saved it from destruction, allowing its forces to recuperate and airfields to be restored. It was a terrible price for Londoners to pay, the death toll rose to 2,000 by 10 September. However, 15 September marked the heaviest bombardment of the capital so far – but at a cost to the Luftwaffe of 56 planes. This date, originally designated as the launch for 'Operation Sealion', would prove a turning point in the Battle of Britain, as the German High Command realised that their invasion of Britain would be at an unsustainable cost. Thus, 15 September became Battle of Britain Day. On 17 September, Hitler abandoned 'Operation Sealion' but not until 29 October could Britain breathe a little easier as the stream of German raiding aircraft subsided.

At the start of the Battle of Britain, Fighter Command was outnumbered four to one by the Luftwaffe and faced a better-equipped German force that was battle-hardened and had superior aerial tactics. Both sides revealed, in almost equal measure, gaps in their knowledge and understanding of the opposition. The Germans generally under-estimated Britain's will to defend its shores and over-estimated the RAF's defensive capability. Additionally, German intelligence was inferior to British, which began to experience the benefit of ULTRA – the British code name for the breaking of the German Enigma encoding system. On its part, RAF Fighter Command over-estimated Luftwaffe strength and will, but it is easy to understand why this happened, when the attrition of such huge numbers of aircraft continued for so long. In reality, however, the Luftwaffe was also close to exhaustion by September 1940.

The milestone date for the end of the Battle of Britain – 29 October – was arbitrary to some extent, as Britain would continue to experience the German Blitz until the early summer of 1941. Nevertheless, at this point in the war, it was possible to begin counting the cost of this decisive battle: during the Battle of Britain from 10 July to 31 October, Britain lost 1,065 aircraft (including 1,004 fighters) and 544 pilots; German losses numbered 1,922 aircraft (including 879 fighters, 80 Stukas and 881 bombers). British civilian losses in the Blitz that ended in May 1941 soared to over 40,000 killed and 50,000 injured. German Luftwaffe losses from August 1940 until March 1941 were nearly 3,000 aircraft lost and 3,363 aircrew killed, with 2,117 wounded and 2,641 taken prisoner.

The Battle of Britain presents a vivid pictorial record of how Britons experienced this chapter of the war through more than 200 wonderfully detailed photographs from the *Daily Mail* archive, fully restored to a previously unseen quality. These stunning photographs are accompanied by their contemporary captions and annotations to give a comprehensive portrait of life during the greatest military threat Britain had faced for centuries.

The Few

The gratitude of every home in our Island, in our Empire, and indeed throughout the world, except in the abodes of the guilty, goes out to the British airmen who, undaunted by odds, unwearied in their constant challenge and mortal danger, are turning the tide of the World War by their prowess and their devotion. Never in the field of human conflict was so much owed by so many to so few. All hearts go out to the fighter pilots, whose brilliant actions we see with our own eyes day after day; but we must never forget that all the time, night after night, month after month, our bomber squadrons travel far into Germany, find their targets in the darkness by the highest navigational skill, aim their attacks, often under the heaviest fire, often with serious loss, with deliberate careful discrimination, and inflict shattering blows upon the whole of the technical and war-making structure of the Nazi power. On no part of the Royal Air Force does the weight of the war fall more heavily than on the daylight bombers, who will play an invaluable part in the case of invasion and whose unflinching zeal it has been necessary in the meanwhile on numerous occasions to restrain.

Prime Minister Winston Churchill
Speech to the House of Commons on 20 August 1940

Dawning of the Blitzkrieg

Above: A dawn reconnaissance mission for a squadron of RAF Hurricanes in November 1939. Unwritten rules of engagement existed in the early months of the war, with the aim of avoiding unnecessary civilian deaths. The blitz-bombing of Rotterdam on 14 May to bring the Netherlands into submission changed the rulebook. Aerial reconnaissance provided vital strategic information and RAF planes were adapted to house cameras to capture troop movements and defensive installations.

Opposite: Jubilant RAF airmen group around a captured Luftwaffe Dornier set out for expert examination in a shed in France. The RAF presence in France was significant at the start of the war. albeit outnumbered by opposing Luftwaffe forces. Despite this, RAF fighter planes had considerable success against German bombers.

Testing early days of war

Left: Three of 1 Squadron's Hurricanes, make a mock attack on a Fairey Battle light bomber. Training of fighter pilots was a major issue for the RAF which faced battle-hardened Luftwaffe opponents fresh from the Spanish Civil War. Fighter pilots had to rapidly learn vital tactical skills for a wide range of deployment.

Opposite: This Lockheed Hudson was lucky to return to base in May 1940 without any casualties to the crew after a direct hit from German guns over recently invaded Norway. The unarmoured bodywork of World War II aircraft made them highly vulnerable to anti-aircraft fire from the ground as well as from aerial combat.

RAF tactical defence in the Battle for France

Opposite: Aerial dogfights often happened at high altitude; from the ground, fighter planes might appear to be the size of birds, their engines and machine guns inaudible. However, their vapour trails dramatically represented the life and death struggle being played out in the sky.

Above: In May 1940 three more RAF Squadrons reinforced existing units in France followed by a further 32 Hurricanes. But by 17 May, the end of the first week of fighting, only three of the ten Hurricane squadrons were near operational strength. Despite their heavy losses, the Hurricanes had managed to destroy nearly double the number of German aircraft. 501 Squadron, pictured here days after arriving in Northern France, accounted for 15 kills in their first two days.

Meeting the threat of German dive bombers

Opposite: Effective camouflage was essential for all Allied installations and materiel over France because of the Luftwaffe's aerial superiority. Not only did their fighter aircraft dominate the skies, their dive bombers, the legendary Stuka and larger brother the Junkers 88, created havoc well behind the front line of battle. Invisible from the air, this aircraft was ready to take off at a moment's notice.

Above: Airmen of RAF 87 Squadron based in northern France race for their Hurricanes to intercept incoming Luftwaffe aircraft. Within minutes they had to be at combat height and in formation to have the best chance against their already-airborne enemy.

Miraculous escape during the Dunkirk evacuation

Above: Allied soldiers line up on the beach at Dunkirk awaiting evacuation. They waited hours in the sea, sometimes in shoulder-high water. In the nine days from 27 May to 4 June, 338,226 people escaped, including 139,997 French, Polish and Belgian troops, together with a small number of Dutch soldiers, aboard 861 vessels (of which 243 were sunk during the operation).

Opposite: The docks at Dunkirk were too badly damaged to be used but the East and West Moles (sea walls protecting the harbour entrance) remained intact. The officer in charge of the evacuation decided to use the beaches and the East Mole to land the ships. This improvisation increased the number of troops that could be embarked each day, and at the rescue operation's peak, on 31 May, enabled over 68,000 men to be taken off.

Operation Dynamo saves over 300,000 allied troops

Opposite: Dunkirk evacuees walk across several vessels moored side-by-side in the British port. Some manage a grin but most remain dazed from the ordeal of the preceding days in France: the march to the coast under unceasing bombardment from artillery and aircraft. Many feared the reception awaiting them at home, believing they had let their country down.

Above: Although the troops trapped in Dunkirk took a terrible pounding, Operation Dynamo was a miraculous success, aided by Hitler's order to halt the advance of his troops on 26 May, at a point where there was nothing to stop them annihilating the retreating BEF and Allied troops. These three days of grace, before the Fuhrer lifted his order, made a huge difference to the evacuation.

A remnant army

Left: A ship returns from Dunkirk loaded with transport and equipment. Such a photograph encouraged the British public to look positively on the terrible defeat suffered in France. In reality, the BEF had been more or less stripped of its weaponry and transport, thanks to the efficient destruction of retreating troop columns by German fighters and dive-bombers. Much equipment had to be abandoned and destroyed during the retreat.

Opposite: Seamen, whose vessels had been sunk during the evacuation, mingled with troops and wounded as they came ashore. Dry clothes had to be improvised, as did field dressings when normal supplies were unavailable.

Heroes welcomed home from France

Opposite: Spirits quickly lifted as troops began the next stage of their evacuation. Many locations around the United Kingdom had been prepared for the huge numbers of soldiers, many of whom were not English.

Above: A downed aircrew, returning from France, with their distinctive goggles and scarves, put on a cheerful face while handing out cigarettes to the crowd of children mobbing their carriage. One pilot recounted how, having been shot down over France, he returned to his base 19 hours later - via the Dunkirk evacuation!

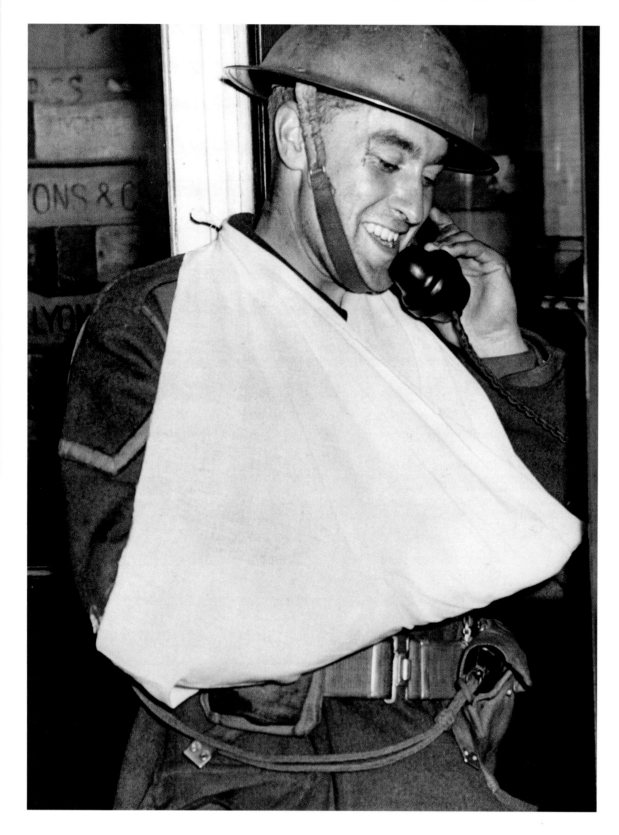

The lucky walking wounded

Left: A Dunkirk evacuee manages the luxury of a phone call; limited by logistics and censorship, letters to and from home took weeks to arrive. The delighted look as he makes contact with home says it all.

Opposite: The hail of artillery and aerial bombardment resulted in many casualties: these soldiers in their field dressings put on a brave face, oblivious to the discomfort of their wounds.

Free from bombardment - respite at last

Above: Unable to sleep properly for many days prior to their evacuation, exhausted servicemen simply lay down and dozed wherever they could - even on the ground here at the reception centre, awaiting their orders.

Opposite: The returning troops in their trains were often met by welcoming children; most soldiers had no contact with home for some time and were desperate to get news to their loved ones that they had survived. Frequently a short message with a name and address would be handed into the crowd in the hope that news would get through.

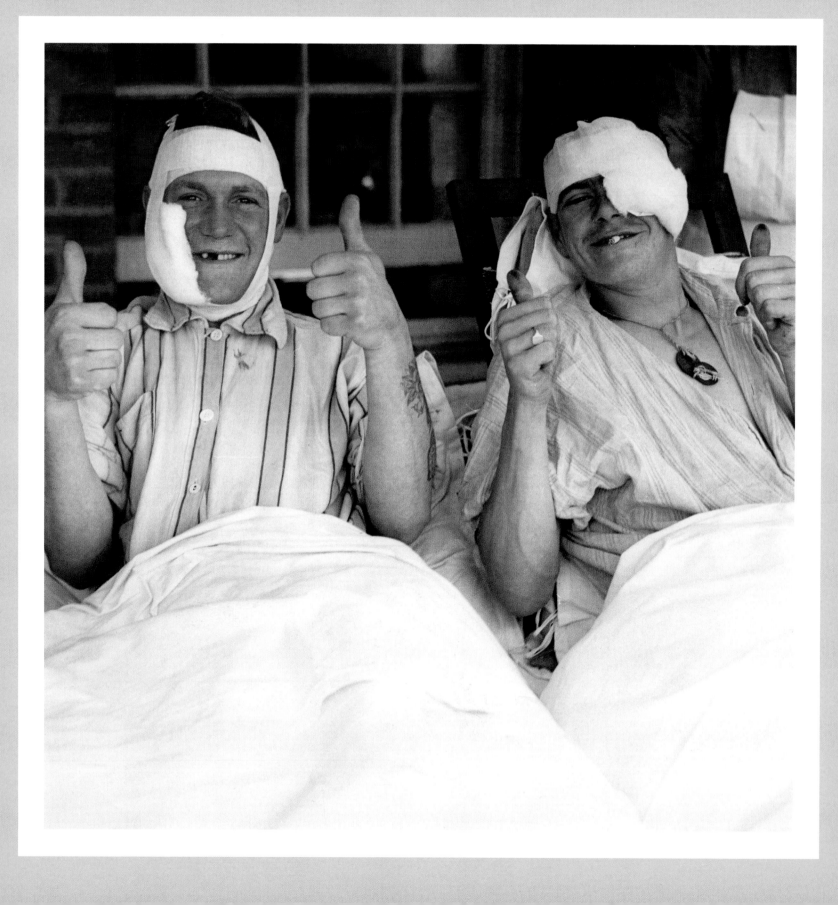

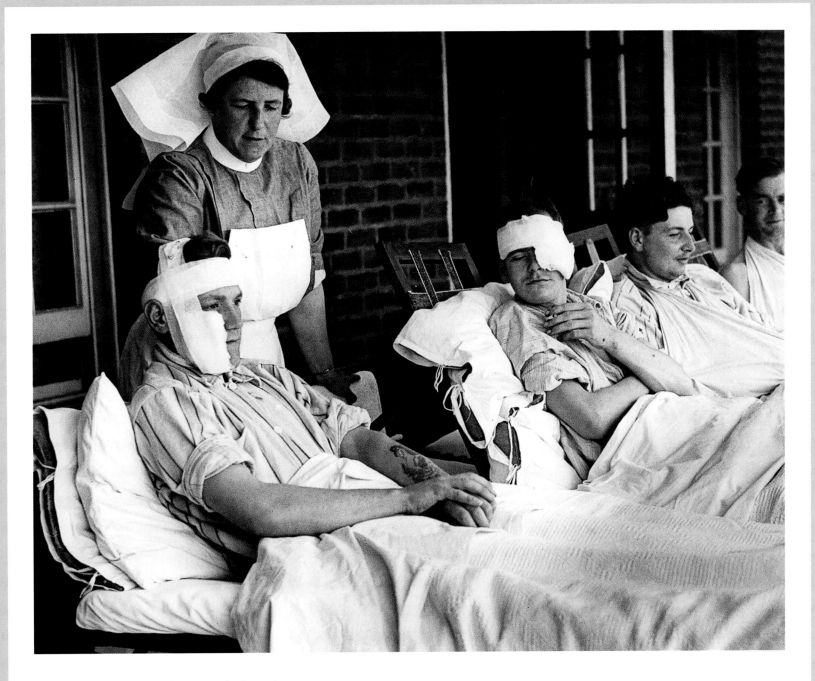

General hospitals care for wounded survivors

Opposite: Convalescing from their wounds in a Hertfordshire hospital, two soldiers give the traditional thumbs-up. Many of the severely wounded were too ill to be moved and had to be left at Dunkirk in the care of volunteer medics.

Above: The flood of wounded soldiers spread around the country. During WWII there were 122 General Hospitals throughout the theatres of war, to look after military wounded. A number of these mobile units returned from northern France before Operation Dynamo but many nurses were evacuated from the Dunkirk beaches. As can be seen, a nursing sister could be as fearsome in her discipline as any NCO.

Pressure increases on RAF bomber crews

Opposite: An aircrew pose in front of their badly damaged Avro Anson bomber, hit by anti-aircraft fire on a reconnaissance mission Despite wing and engine damage, shell-splintered fuselage and shot-out tyres they managed to return home without injury.

Above: During the Battle for France and the Battle of Britain, RAF bombers were kept busy attacking targets in the heart of Germany as well as in France. A bomber crew nonchalantly recount their narrow escape in March 1940 when, off course and short of fuel, they made an unscheduled landing to get their bearings. Asking a local if they were in France, they were told 'No, Germany'. They quickly took off and returned to tell the tale!

Optimism in face of increasing odds against the RAF

Above: Crew-members of a bomber flight stationed in France since the outbreak of war. The RAF's main bomber aircraft for this force was the Bristol Blenheim, a lightly armed, slow moving aircraft which, despite valiant efforts, was no match for German fighter attack, resulting in appalling losses.

Opposite: Pilots of 501 Squadron, the first Auxiliary Fighter Squadron to join the Advanced Air Striking Force (AASF) in France, unwind after their latest dogfight in the middle of May. In the background, future RAF Ace, Flt Sergeant 'Ginger' Lacey.

The Luftwaffe's deadly fighter aircraft

Above: The Luftwaffe's proven fighter plane at the start of the war was the Messerschmitt Bf 109. It became the most produced fighter aircraft in history with a total of 33,984 built until production stopped in April 1945. The RAF's Spitfire was a good match in many respects, but performance was still dictated by the pilot's skill, knowledge of his own plane and the key strengths and weaknesses of the machine he was fighting against.

Opposite: The RAF had been updating its combat aircraft since the 1930s, but they were untested in war so defects and weaknesses remained to be resolved. These Blackburn Skuas, executing a textbook move in V-formation, were already out of date when deployed in the Fleet Air Arm. The RAF had to rapidly revise their formation and dogfight tactics, as well as addressing the design limitations of their aircraft.

Protecting the pilot

Opposite: Rapid rearming and refuelling were critical for the RAF, which flew many more sorties in France and during the Battle of Britain than its German opponents. A Spitfire at this time carried 300 rounds of ammunition for each of its 8 Browning .303 machine guns housed in the wings. The thin wing profile made rearming more laborious than the Hurricane. The Messerschmitt Bf 109 carried more ammunition for its machine guns; RAF pilots had to count every burst in seconds, having less than 20 seconds total supply.

Right: In a training session in Scotland, early in 1940, RAF airmen observe a demonstration of the Irvin parachute which had become standard equipment some years before. Leslie Irvin, an American, set up his parachute and flying jacket factory in Letchworth in the 1930s. The kit comprised a harness and attached parachute pack.

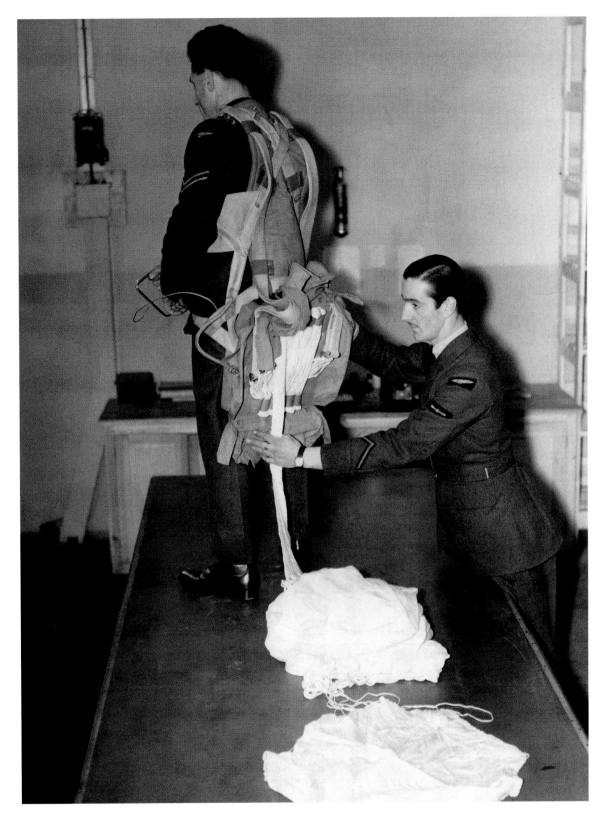

Spitfires inspire confidence

Opposite: The appearance of the Supermarine Spitfire in the air over France and England gave confidence to civilians and troops alike. The sleek beauty and effortless speed of the state-of-the-art fighter planes were first demonstrated in Europe in a confidence-building flypast on Bastille Day, 14 July 1939. These six aircraft roared over the leading units of slow-moving bombers, as they passed over the Arc de Triomphe.

Above: The vital task of spotting aircraft was a 24-hour task, with observers staring into the sky for long hours, day and night. Special spotter chairs were made for the purpose, seen here being used during the day in France; they were also used by night-time searchlight crews.

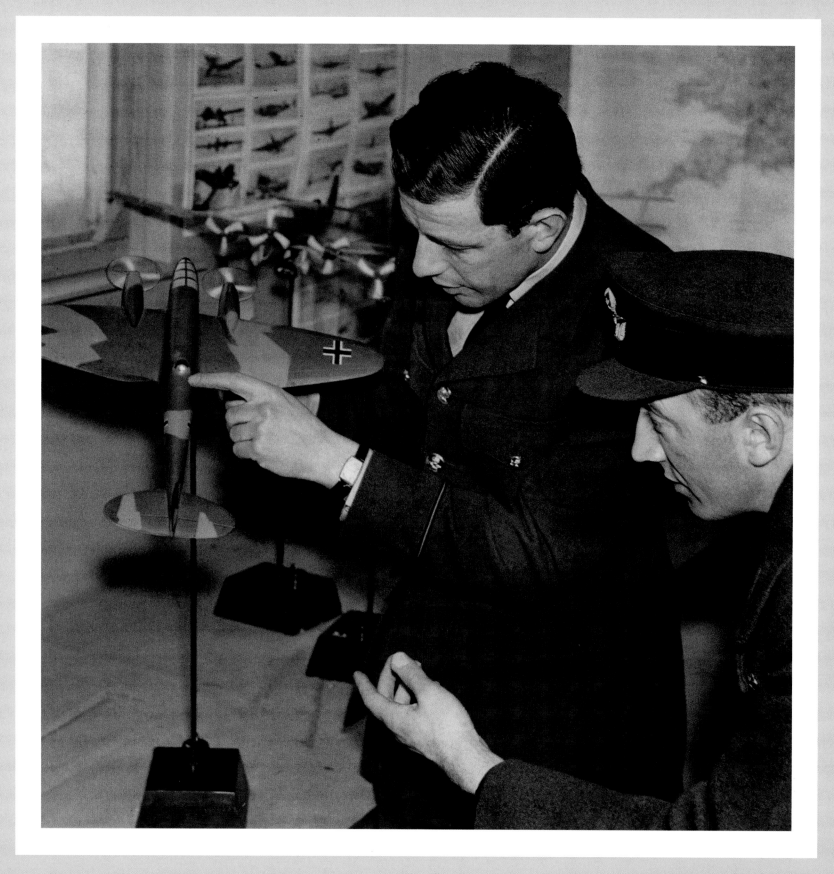

Know your enemy

Opposite: The swift identification of aircraft was a vital skill for both aircrews and ground personnel. Under varying light conditions, it was easy to mistake friend and foe. Both sides frequently made adaptations to their aircraft - either in the factory or at the base - and it was essential to keep track of these, incorporating the information into training to avoid nasty surprises.

Left: The billets provided for RAF aircrew in France varied but were often little better than makeshift. These pilots sleep soundly in their clothes in a farm outbuilding with their essentials close to hand: wellingtons, gas masks and steel helmets.

Boats of the Dunkirk flotilla come home

Opposite: In the aftermath of the Dunkirk evacuation, naval personnel were released for much-deserved leave. The war effort would demand their early return, however: months of dangerous work lay ahead to ensure regular shipments from overseas allies reached the British at home.

Above: The boats used for the evacuation came from all around Britain. Some, like the river cruisers shown here, quickly returned to their domestic berths where they spent the rest of the war, with little fuel available to permit their use. Others were kept in service for training or other purposes designated by the Royal Navy.

Winston leads the nation

Left and opposite: The overwhelming speed of the German war machine as it moved West, and Prime Minister Chamberlain's general failure to effect any resistance, frustrated Winston Churchill who was appointed First Lord of the Admiralty at the declaration of war. In the years before the war, Churchill was critical of Chamberlain's lack of preparation against the obvious rearming of Germany by Hitler's Nazis. On 10 May, Chamberlain resigned and recommended Churchill as the man to head an all-party war government. He accepted the invitation from George VI and immediately stepped into the role, much to the relief of the nation. On 13 May, his first great speech to Parliament sounded around the nation with the immortal words "I have nothing to offer but blood, toil, tears and sweat."

In addition to being Prime Minister, Churchill appointed himself Minister of Defence, giving him control of Britain's armed forces. These pictures demonstrate his ability and determination to play both roles to full effect.

Are we downhearted?

Opposite: In April 1940 Winston Churchill pays a visit to one of Britain's dockyards, primary targets for Luftwaffe bombers. Addressing the assembled workers, he questioned, 'Are we downhearted?' to be greeted with a resounding, 'No!' This was a catchphrase from a song that was used throughout the Battle of Britain and the Blitz.

Above: Adolf Hitler in conference with Reichsmarschall Hermann Goering (2nd left), commander of the Luftwaffe. Hitler made him personally responsible for defeating the RAF prior to Operation Sealion, the planned invasion of Britain in September 1940.

WAAFs man the barrage balloons

Opposite and above: Members of the Women's Auxiliary Air Force (WAAFs) manoeuvre an anti-aircraft barrage balloon into position. Tethered balloons had been used in WWI as observation platforms for artillery aiming, giving rise to the expression 'the balloon goes up'. The aerodynamic shape was developed to keep them more manageable in the wind. By the middle of 1940, there were about 1,400 deployed around the country, a third of them assigned to London. Their purpose was to inhibit dive bombing and force aircraft to fly within the height range of anti-aircraft guns which were not agile enough to engage diving or low-flying aircraft. The combined effect forced enemy bombers to keep above both balloons and anti-aircraft shells, thus decreasing their bombing accuracy.

Skill, patience and strength

Opposite: The balloons could be maintained in fixed positions or moved around as required. When not in action, they were tethered close to the ground and then released manually or by winch to their operating altitude to meet attack. Balloon Command was based at Stanmore, Middlesex close to Fighter Command's HQ at Bentley Priory. The balloons were produced, along with the hydrogen gas they needed, in purpose-built hangars at RAF Cardington in Bedfordshire.

Above: Barrage balloons were very large - just over 18m in length and just under 8m in diameter; getting them inflated as well as into position required patience and skill. At first it was doubted that WAAFs would have the necessary strength, but these fears were quickly dispelled.

Coastal Command defends Britain's shipping lanes

Opposite: Shipping and submarine movements are tracked in the control room of RAF Coastal Command, which provided aerial protection of Allied shipping from both the Luftwaffe and German U-boats. It received much less glory than its Fighter and Bomber Command cousins. In the first phase of the Battle of Britain, the so-called 'Kanalkampf', from 10 July to 11 August, Luftwaffe attacks focused on shipping in the English Channel and the North Sea.

Above: Naval anchorages were well protected by barrage balloons. At a cost of six lost aircraft, the Luftwaffe destroyed 40 of them over Dover on a late August raid, only to find in reconnaissance next day, 34 of them were replaced. Such rapid recovery was seen as a significant obstacle and another surprise to German intelligence. Using just rifle fire, this crew were credited with downing the Bf 109 that destroyed their balloon.

Volunteers of the Observer Corps watch the skies

Opposite: The Observer Corps was manned by civilian volunteers throughout the country to detect and record the movement of aircraft across the skies. Using a sighting tool called the Micklethwaite post instrument which was positioned over a locally oriented map grid, accurate height and position could be reported. Here noted Welsh tenor Mr Watkins relays information on his telephone headset that is given to him by architect Mr Pointon Taylor.

Right: Large employers and institutions assigned staff as 'roof spotters', tasked with warning their colleagues to seek shelter in the event of enemy aircraft approaching. Here three smart-suited employees keep watch on the roof of the American Embassy in London.

Vigilance is provided by both sexes and all ages

Left: Two Girl Guides scan the sky from the roof of the Association's HQ building in London; one watches while the other holds her whistle in readiness to give the signal of attack.

Opposite: Spotters stationed on the roof of the *Daily Mail*'s Northcliffe House, Fleet Street, London, are silhouetted against the tracery of dogfight vapour trails.

Total concentration grips an Observer Corps control room

Above: Inside an Observer Corps control room, 'plotters' move counters across an area map tracking incoming information from clusters of observation posts. 'Tellers' overlooking the plotters are responsible for liaising with fellow control rooms and local defence organisations as well as their contact at Fighter Command HQ at Bentley Priory.

Opposite: Air Chief Marshal Dowding said of the Observer Corps; It is important to note that at this time they constituted the whole means of tracking enemy raids once they had crossed the coastline. Their work throughout was quite invaluable. Without it the air-raid warning systems could not have been operated and inland interceptions would rarely have been made.'

All eyes on the skies

Opposite: Steel helmets marked 'OC' or a beret and a distinctive armband were the only identification of the Corps during the Battle of Britain. As a result of their efforts during the Battle, the Observer Corps was granted the title 'Royal' by King George VI and became a uniformed volunteer branch of the RAF from April 1941 for the remainder of its existence.

Above: Women of the Auxiliary Territorial Service (ATS) on observation duty at an anti-aircraft battery. Although they didn't handle the armament they were trained to use the rangefinders and accurately identify enemy aircraft.

Women of the ATS join the gun crews

Above: From spring 1940, it became quite common for women of the ATS to be deployed in mixed anti-aircraft, or 'ack-ack' crews. Like their opposite numbers in the Observer Corps, they were on duty 24 hours a day in their exposed batteries, whatever the weather.

Opposite: The first line of defence against incoming German aircraft was the coastal batteries alerted by the RDF Chain (early radar) that silently guarded Britain. Here, in the northwest of England, a member of this 4-inch gun crew sights up a target.

Anti-aircraft emplacements spring up

Above: From 26th August, the Luftwaffe moved their focus to RAF airfields in the next phase of the Battle of Britain; here Welsh AA gunners race to their battery on the evening of 29th August to defend their base against one of the worst attacks by the Luftwaffe.

Opposite: A seven-man anti-aircraft crew in action in their hastily positioned emplacements, with no protection other than a chest-high wall of sandbags. While the majority of enemy planes were shot down by fighter engagement, ack-ack fire broke up bomber formations and reduced their accuracy. During the Battle of Britain, around 300 Luftwaffe planes were shot down by guns such as these.

Armed and ready

Opposite: After setting the fuzes on these 3.7 inch (94mm) anti-aircraft shells, the officer chalks the timing on the casing. Firing at around 10-20 rounds per minute this row of shells would give 2 minutes of concentrated fire. The shells weighed 28 pounds (12.7kg) and had a ceiling range of 30,000 feet (9,000m). This heavy ordnance had an impressive airburst but lighter weaponry with a faster rate of fire could have been more effective. The guns were in use day and night and had to be scrupulously maintained. In the background one of the crew cleans the barrel.

Above: By the height of the Battle of Britain there were around 1,100 AA guns placed around the UK, 400 of them assigned to the protection of London. During the Battle, 260,000 high-explosive rounds were fired at enemy air formations. The heavy discharge of the guns and aerial explosions of their shells, combined with news pictures such as this, reassured civilians as they took shelter.

Watching, listening, waiting

Opposite: The frequency and suddenness of attack during this phase of the Battle required constant vigilance; looking out for the smallest dot in the sky was a day and night occupation, especially at the RAF's airfields.

Right: World War II brought many military innovations; almost on a daily basis, weaponry and production was improved. This 'listening' device was designed to pick up approaching aircraft noise and was particularly important at night when searchlights would give away ground positions and provide a target for the German bombers. Searchlights were plentiful during the Battle but were used specifically to aid AA targeting.

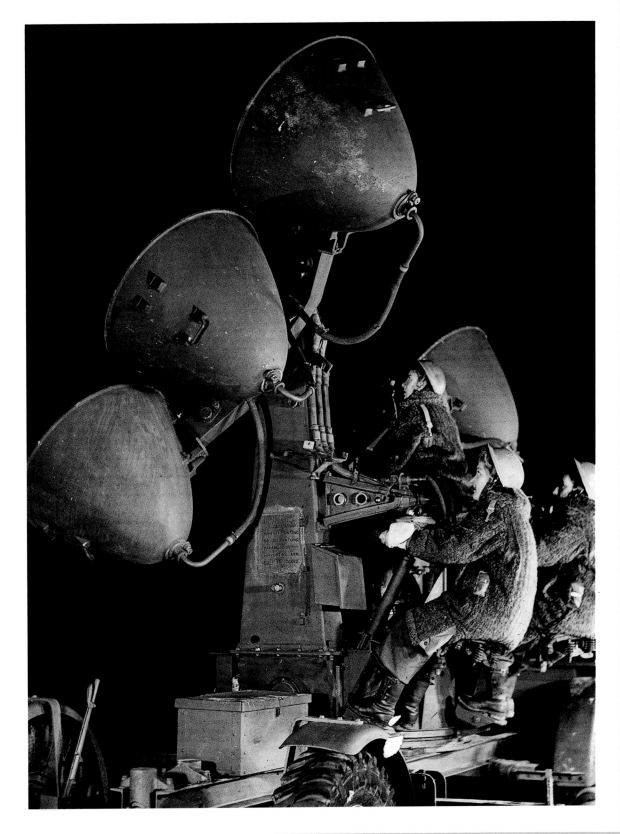

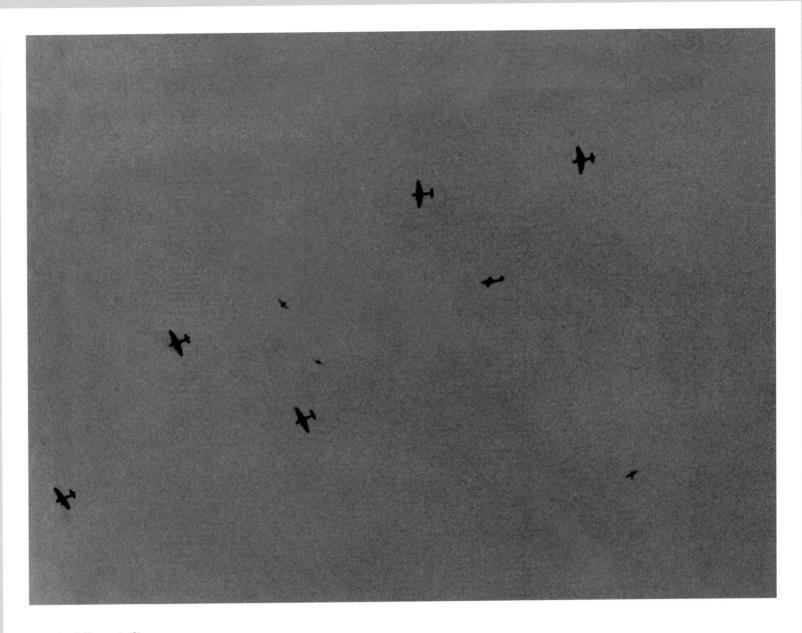

Bombs fall on civilians

Opposite: A typical suburban street devastated by bombing in the early hours of 15th July 1940; a scene of extraordinary calm shows workers repairing a water main and the bomb damage to the road while ARP officers converse in the background. The close-packed terraces increased the efficiency of the bombs, while fire from incendiaries could quickly spread from house to house. From 7 September, the Luftwaffe moved their main attention from the RAF airfields to a campaign of terror delivered from the air; this marked the beginning of the Blitz and the final phase of the Battle of Britain.

Above: On the afternoon of 14th August, an enemy bomber formation is intercepted by RAF Hurricanes off the coast of Kent. Without protective fighter cover the bombers were sitting ducks. This photograph shows RAF fighters breaking into their dive attacks from above the German formation, which fled back to base in the face of this determined attack.

Random damage

Opposite: Under attack from British fighters, the laden German bombers had to jettison their bombs or find an available target quickly and hope to escape. The power of the ordnance is visible in this enormous crater.

Above: Even after unloading their bombs, German aircraft were still vulnerable, as the debris shown in this photograph reveals. The only recognisable part of this shot-down plane is one of its guns.

In search of safety

Opposite: Women and children take cover at the side of a road as enemy planes fly overhead.

Above: On 12 August Goering launched 'Adlerangriff,' or Eagle Attack, which moved focus onto land from the Channel, aiming bombs first at radar installations and coastal airfields then gradually moving further inland. Uncertain weather conditions inhibited the German attack, but nevertheless the number of planes was vast. On 15th August, the weather cleared late morning to give perfect conditions for the 800 bombers and 1,000 fighters that were to assemble over France to begin the day's action. By the end of the day many targets had been bombed, but at a terrible price: the Luftwaffe lost 75 aircraft against the RAF's loss of 17 pilots killed and 30 aircraft shot down. The day was named Black Thursday by the Luftwaffe.

Our boys are winning!

Left: Aerial battles provided amazing spectacles for the people of Britain. Here city workers in London watch a series of dogfights during their lunch hour. Their expressions give a clear indication of which side is winning on this occasion. Other daylight raids were more terrifying as seemingly endless formations of enemy aircraft appeared over Britain.

On 16th August, Churchill visited 11 Group's HQ at RAF Uxbridge; in the control room, witnessing the relentless pressure on the RAF, he was chastened - asking that his escort should not speak to him. From that experience, came the speech that he made to Parliament on 20th August containing the immortal words, 'Never in the field of human conflict has so much been owed by so many to so few.' Thereafter, the men of RAF Fighter Command would be known as 'The Few'.

Hellfire Corner

Opposite: The Prime Minister pays a visit to Hellfire Corner: the port of Ramsgate was one of the seaside towns of Kent closest to France and therefore most exposed to attack from the Luftwaffe, who used the distinctive coastline here as a navigation aid. If the bombers failed to find their targets or had to dash back to their mainland base they freely jettisoned their bombs here. For the nation, Ramsgate's association with Operation Dynamo was a powerful, recent memory.

Above: Spitfires of 65 (East India) Squadron stand with their engines running in a state of maximum readiness, able to take off at any moment. Four states of operational readiness were normally maintained by the squadrons of Fighter Command: 'Released', meaning they were unavailable; 'Available', meaning that the aircraft could be ready for take off within a certain number of minutes; 'Readiness', meaning awaiting orders to take off; 'Standby', meaning that pilots are in their aircraft pointing into the wind with their engines running.

Scramble: action stations!

Opposite: Pilots of the West Lancashire RAF Squadron race to their waiting aircraft after they receive the call to 'action stations'; their mascot, Joker, joins in the spirit of the scramble.

Above: From the expression on the faces of these scrambling RAF pilots it's hard to believe they were on their way to an experience which would terrify normal people. On this day, 1st September 1940, they were launched to reinforce already engaged squadrons in the southeast.

Intercepting a dawn raid

Above: An early morning scramble turns 611 Spitfire Squadron into a hive of activity, with some pilots already in their cockpits whilst others run to their aircraft. Their engines would have been started by the ground crew, who would also assist the pilots - and their cumbersome parachute packs - into their seats. There would be last-minute checks after strapping in and connecting the oxygen supply, then chocks away and take off.

Opposite: In Kent, debris fell continually from the skies: shrapnel from shells, pieces of aircraft and sometimes whole planes. As long as it was German there were no complaints. One enterprising farmer tried to raise money for the Spitfire Fund by charging locals 6d 'to see the only field in Kent without a German aircraft in it'.

Calm before the storm

Right: The summer of 1940 was balmy, with many days of sunshine. Aircrews fighting for their life one moment could be recuperating at the margins of their grassy runways soon after, ready at an instant to return to battle. However, the weather wasn't good the whole time. At the beginning of August, Eagle Day - the day the Luftwaffe began its real assault on the RAF - was quite seriously delayed by bad flying conditions, finally launching in earnest on 13th August, after low cloud cleared in the early afternoon. Confusion in the German command made the planned attack less effective; the Luftwaffe were surprised by the firm resolve and force of the defending RAF who lost 13 aircraft in the air compared with 47 German planes.

Wreckage

Opposite: Clouds of black smoke pour out of this downed Luftwaffe bomber, shot down near the coast of southern England on its flight back to France.

Above: Little remains of this burnt-out German plane to identify it. Shot down over the Thames Estuary, it was a casualty of one of the ferocious dogfights waged daily in this aerial corridor that funnelled incoming enemy aircraft to their bombing targets. British fighter planes were able to greet them in the air thanks to radar and the efficient communication structures administered under Dowding's Fighter Command.

Closing for the kill

Above: A Spitfire goes in for the kill. Already crippled and trailing smoke, this Heinkel 111 is seconds away from ditching in the Channel. This photograph shows how close RAF fighters had to get to their targets to make their ammunition effective. Their relatively light machine guns were eventually upgraded to include heavier 20mm cannon.

Opposite: Hurricanes speed on their way to intercept enemy aircraft on 29th July. Three planes are in the classic V formation. The others are adopting the increasingly favoured 'finger four', which paired planes as two couples. With the lead pilot in attack, his wingman would keep a lookout for attacking aircraft from above and from the direction of the sun.

Crashed Heinkel

Above: A Hurricane pilot flies over the burning Heinkel he has just shot down while it was returning from a bombing raid on London in September 1940. It was common for fighters to 'waggle their wings' in a jubilant gesture of victory. In this flat open field can be seen primitive obstacles to landing enemy aircraft; the threat of imminent invasion was in the minds of the entire population.

Opposite: The Hurricane of Sub-Lt Begg, who joined 151 Squadron from the Fleet Air Arm on 1st July 1940. With the damage sustained to the tail section, it's remarkable that the plane was able to return and make a safe landing. The construction of the control surfaces is revealed: damage like this could be repaired and the plane would quickly return to service. Begg was shot down and wounded in August, and then reported missing in action in November 1942, aged 25.

Black Thursday

Opposite: A burnt-out Dornier that failed to reach its London destination is guarded until the wreck can be assessed by intelligence experts. Local people were keen to collect souvenirs from the downed planes before they were removed to recycling centres.

Above: Two German planes lie wrecked on a beach on the south-east coast. The worst day of the Battle for the Bf 110 was 15 August 1940, 'Black Thursday', when nearly 30 Bf 110s were shot down, the equivalent of an entire Gruppe. Between the 16th-17th August a further 23 Bf 110s were shot down.

Taking apart a Junkers 88

Above: A downed Junkers 88 that landed in one piece provides useful intelligence for an Air Ministry team. Ju 88 losses over Britain amounted to 313 machines between July-October 1940. Do 17 and He 111 losses for the same period amounted to 132 and 252 machines respectively.

Opposite: The unmistakable profile of Winston Churchill, captured by the press near a coastal defence installation which he was inspecting on 9 August 1940. The threat of invasion was at its height and British reconnaissance showed the large numbers of invasion barges being assembled in the French channel ports.

September crisis for the RAF

Above: Night attacks by 120 Luftwaffe bombers were followed by dawn raids on 2 September, with continual attacks by hundreds of enemy bombers with fighter escorts in waves throughout the day. Many bombs found their targets, making Eastchurch airfield in Kent non-operational. Despite their losses, such as this downed Bf 109, the German attrition was steadily weakening Fighter Command who had flown 700 sorties that day alone.

Opposite: RAF pilots kept their tally of kills painted next to the cockpit; these two groundcrew give the much-used gestures of optimism - the thumbs-up and V-sign - for the addition of 2 bombers to this Spitfire's record.

Collecting the debris

Left: An RAF airman holds up part of a Dornier's propeller; the shot-down aircraft destroyed a garden outbuilding when it crashed in mid-August.

Opposite: Workmen carry a section of fuselage belonging to a downed German bomber. They are adding the latest wreckage to a scrap heap covering 20 acres, stacked high with recovered debris, which was then recycled into British aircraft and weapon production.

Continuing German losses

Opposite: Air Ministry officials inspect the wreckage of a Stuka which partially demolished this house after being shot down near the south coast on 15 August. Fortunately, the house was unoccupied at the time.

Above: Only one member of the four-man crew of this Heinkel bomber survived when it was brought down on a night mission at the beginning of September.

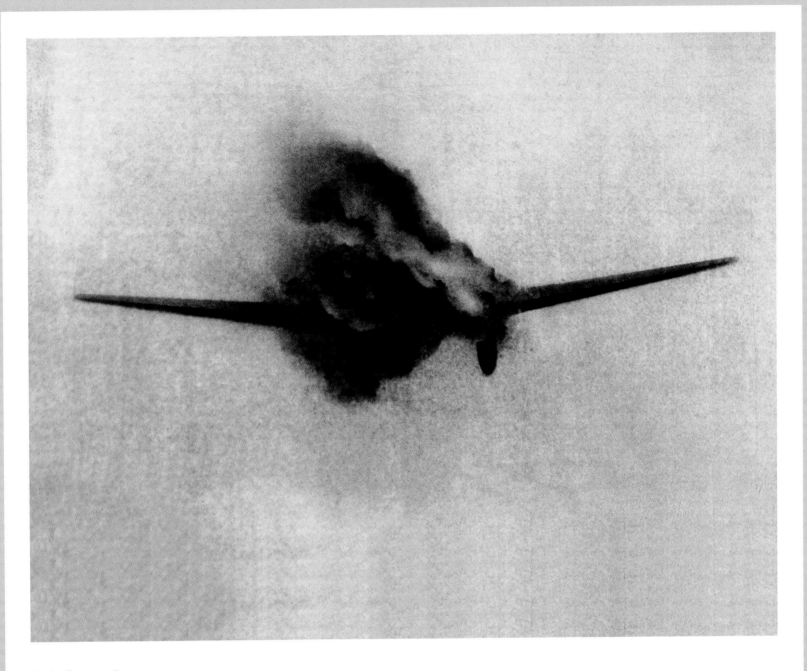

Early devastation

Opposite: Late on 30 April, a Heinkel 111 with a damaged engine crash-landed amongst houses at Clacton-on-Sea, Essex. The aircraft was laying mines in the English Channel and seems to have been attacked by the RAF. It was still loaded with high explosive and, after crashing, first exploded then burst into flames. The four aircrew were killed along with Mr & Mrs Gill, whose house was obliterated. A further 156 people were injured, some of them seriously. This was the first intimation for Britain of the damage that was likely to be caused in the Battle ahead. The event was widely publicised to show that the emergency services were ready to meet the challenge of the enemy.

Above: The last moments of this crippled Heinkel are captured by the camera, synchronised with the guns on board the Hurricane responsible for shooting it down.

Shattered wrecks

Opposite: The crumpled cockpit of this downed Dornier bomber is barely recognisable. One of 78 Luftwaffe aircraft claimed by the RAF as destroyed on 13 August, giving a six-day running tally of 269. The figures were somewhat exaggerated to counter Germany's overstatement of success in the daily propaganda war.

Above: Badly shot up on 12 August, this Bf 109 crash-landed in a Kent cornfield, almost intact. The wounded pilot managed to get out of the plane but covered no more than 50 yards before he was captured by a sergeant of the Royal Engineers.

More than a 1000 sorties in one day by the RAF

Opposite: The tail wheel is the only recognisable part of this wrecked German fighter plane shot down above the outskirts of London on 30 August, another gruelling day for Fighter Command, in which it flew 1,054 sorties - the highest total of any day in the Battle of Britain, bringing the RAF close to the limits of endurance.

Above: Unusual luck for the rifles of London's Home Guard when they returned the machine-gun fire of this low-flying Dornier on 19 August. To the surprise and delight of the defenders, the bomber crashed soon after. Bullet holes in the fuselage are clearly visible. By 31 July, 1.5m civilians joined the Local Defence Volunteers, which was formed on 14th May and was 'christened' the 'Home Guard' in Churchill's broadcast of 23 July.

Luftwaffe graveyard

Above: A Bf 109, carrying the same markings as the one shown on p107, has been transported to the scrapheap for recycling or spare parts for the reconstruction that sometimes took place. Already the guns have been removed from under the engine cowling, but these airmen have arrived to take the dismantled Bf 109 to a public display to raise money for the Spitfire Fund.

Opposite: The combined effect of high explosive and aviation fuel could have devastating results. This downed German machine is reduced to ashes after falling in woodland in the south of England on 13th August. Fire was an ever-present threat to all airmen, strapped into a small space high in the air, surrounded by highly flammable liquid.

Crashed JU 88

Above: Soldiers guarding this crash-landed Ju 88 check the bullet holes in its oil-spattered wing. It was downed by RAF fighters patrolling the south coast on 14 August.

Opposite: A crashed Bf 109 is buried in the ground after nose-diving to earth when shot down by Hurricanes on 2 September.

Burnt to ash

Opposite: In late August, airmen carry away part of the fuselage of a downed Ju 88. Wreckage parts were sometimes put on display to the public to emphasise RAF successes against the Luftwaffe and to raise money for new planes.

Above: On the South Downs of England, nothing more than white ash and some tangled metal marks the spot where this Ju 88 crashed and burned out, killing all the crew on board - another casualty of the early days of Adlerangriff.

Continuing German losses

Opposite and above: Two Ju 88s meet very different fates when downed by the RAF in August 1940: the more fortunate, opposite, stayed in one piece when it belly-landed near the south coast, probably because it had jettisoned fuel and bombs before setting down. The one above broke up in the air, with little chance of survival for the crew.

Somewhere in England...

Opposite: Hurricanes in Readiness at Biggin Hill, formed up for take off at any moment, each of them hooked up to the accumulator ('trolley-ack') used to start their engine. Ground crew pass the time chatting in the middle of the airfield. Scenes of calm like this could be shattered by German bombs which caused enormous craters; these were invariably filled in with amazing speed to get the airfield operational. The original photograph, which was published in a national newspaper, had the building at the rear touched out in case it provided information for the enemy.

Above: The wounded pilot has already bailed out of this Bf 109 diving to destruction in the Kent fields. Watching him parachute to safety were hop-pickers from the East End of London, many of whom had lost family members and their homes in the bombing raids in recent weeks.

Spitfire pioneers

Above: Pilots of No 19 Squadron, RAF Duxford scramble for their Spitfires. The first Spitfire was flown into Duxford, Cambridgeshire, on 4th August 1938 by Jeffrey Quill, Supermarine's chief test pilot. Theirs was the first squadron to fly the Spitfire, supplied to them in 1938. By September 1940, six squadrons of Hurricanes and Spitfires were based at Duxford and nearby Fowlmere, providing a defensive hub for Air Vice-Mashal Leigh-Mallory's 12 Group.

Opposite: As this picture shows, RAF pilots needed considerable stamina: sorties might begin at dawn with an adrenalin-fuelled run to their aircraft, laden down with their flying equipment. At the peak of the Battle, they would continue flying sorties as long as they could keep awake and had an airworthy machine. They were known to bale out of a doomed plane, be picked up and then immediately return to combat. Many in their crippled aircraft preferred to glide to earth in forced landings, especially when over the Channel.

Anti-aircraft fire bursts in the sky

Opposite: As a formation of 23 German aircraft passes overhead, deadly AA erupts in the sky. Fighter Command claimed 13 of them were shot down on 19th August; the remainder jettisoned their bombs and turned back without reaching their target.

Above: This rather blurred shot from a Spitfire's gun camera shows a Dornier plummeting to the ground in a trail of smoke. The camera gun helped to confirm 'kills', providing pictures that could be used in intelligence and training.

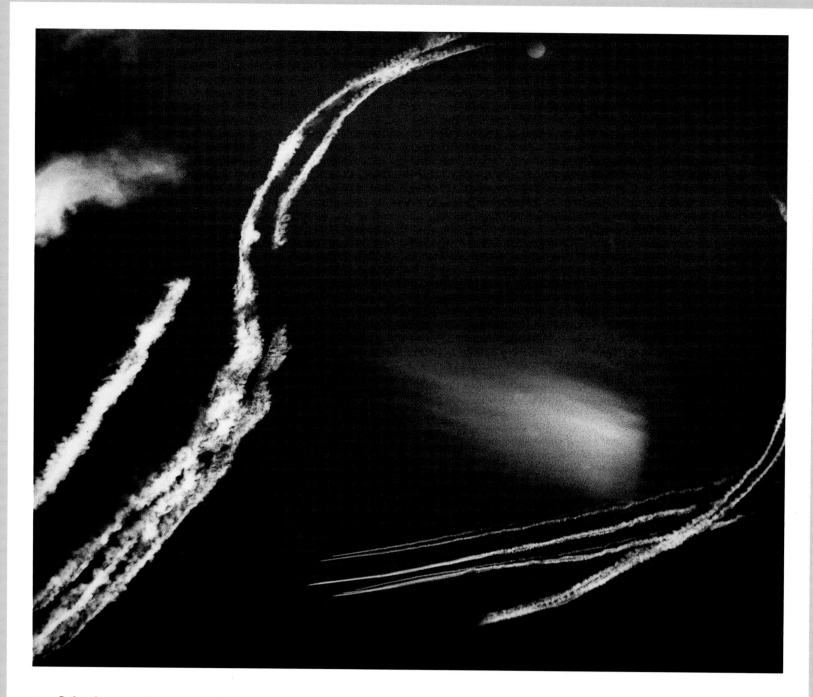

Dogfights leave trails across the sky

Above: Vapour trails leave an account of the dramatic manoeuvres during the high altitude dogfights.

Opposite: German airmen who died on 13th August 1940 (Eagle Day) are buried in this Surrey cemetery with their countrymen. Aircrews on either side had very differing views on their enemy and could show great gallantry towards each other or steely ruthlessness - especially when 'dealing' with baled-out men hanging on parachutes.

MAJ A SCHEUPLEIN
GERMAN AIR FORCE

LT. W. BRINKBAUMER
GERMAN AIR FORCE
13.8.40

On show to the public

Above: This Junkers 88 bomber is guarded by sentries after being brought down by RAF fighters on Eagle Day. Following a huge, but poorly managed offensive, the Luftwaffe lost 34 aircraft to the RAF's 13. Despite the RAF's best efforts German bombers evaded interception and dropped their deadly loads on Fighter Command's airfields.

Opposite: This Messerschmitt Bf 109 went on public display outside Windsor Castle after crash-landing in Windsor Great Park. The King and Queen with their two daughters spent much of the Battle in the Castle. Queen Elizabeth was Commander in Chief of the ATS and Princess Elizabeth was a member, training as a mechanic.

Downed Messerschmitts raise money for the Spitfire Fund

Above: Fund-raising to buy new planes for the RAF led to shot-down Luftwaffe aircraft going on display: for sixpence the public could examine this Bf 110 at close quarters. The fuselage decoration here most carefully excludes the Republic of Ireland from its target!

Opposite: RAF recovery specialists remove the 'little devil' fuselage decoration as they prepare the shot-down Bf 109 to be taken away to the scrap depot.

Luftwaffe fuselage decoration - 'Nose Art'

Opposite: A sheet metal worker removes a fuselage decoration of Mickey Mouse on a Bf109 scheduled for breaking. A Condor squadron of Bf109's adopted Mickey as a decoration in the Spanish Civil War; German Ace Adolf Galland continued to sport one on his personal plane in WWII and it was adopted across his Gruppe.

Above: An airman muses over this unusual fuselage detail on a Bf109 downed on 5th September. A yellow nose cone on the aircraft was believed to denote a Luftwaffe squadron favoured by Goering.

Beaverbrook establishes Civilian Repair Organisation

Opposite: The robust construction of the Hurricane instilled confidence in RAF pilots, but damage like this had to be repaired quickly. During 1940, Lord Beaverbrook, who was the Minister of Aircraft Production, established an organisation in which a number of manufacturers were seconded to repair and overhaul battle damaged Hurricanes. The "Civilian Repair Organisation" also overhauled battle-weary aircraft, which were later sent to training units or to other air forces.

Above: The soldier guarding this downed Bf 109 points out a bullet hole in the cockpit where the pilot had been sitting. The children of Britain often got close to combat or its aftermath, despite widespread evacuation from the cities.

Keeping tally of their kills

Opposite: The kills tally on this shot-down Bf 109 gives an indication of RAF losses and the performance of the German fighter plane. In the early days of the war the Bf 109 clearly had an advantage over the British machines, especially the many outdated craft that were deployed in France.

Above: Clearing the beaches of wrecked German aircraft after Eagle Day, this salvage worker inspects a machine gun in its shattered housing. It came from one of the five planes that ditched on the southeast coast.

Recycling German planes for the British war effort

Above: Viewed through the fuselage of a German fighter, scrap-metal workers break up the metal fabric of downed aircraft to be melted down for manufacturing British planes and weaponry.

Opposite: Tea break at 11 o'clock! Scrapyard workers occupy the seats of the navigator (who also operated the front cannon) and the pilot in the nose of this wrecked Heinkel 111. Plexiglass was the only protection for these two crew and, while it gave them panoramic vision, it made the aircraft highly vulnerable to frontal attack.

A Heinkel 111 captured intact

Opposite: A Heinkel 111 bomber, captured in one piece by the RAF, peeps out from its hangar; it was used for training, propaganda and intelligence. Developed in the early thirties in contravention of the Versailles Treaty, the aircraft originally masqueraded as a commercial airliner then morphed into a reconnaissance plane until finally revealed in its true light as a light-medium bomber. Robust in construction, the machine had up to 5 crew.

Above: Brought safely ashore from the Channel in a rowing boat after bailing out over the sea in late August 1940, this Spitfire pilot reaches terra firma. He had successfully shot down a German bomber when he suffered the same fate. Although equipped with the 'Mae West' flotation vest, pilots were ill-prepared for ditching in the sea and air-sea rescue was not well-supported during the Battle. Germany used dedicated seaplanes and all its pilots were equipped with inflatable rafts in addition to parachutes.

Hawker Hurricanes: the backbone of Britain's defence

Opposite and above: Hawker Hurricanes fly in echelon formation and solo; they were the backbone of the RAF's fighter force during the Battle of Britain. Although outclassed in some respects by the Spitfire and the Bf 109, they had numerous strengths including a rugged and simple build, making them very practical to maintain and repair at their home airfield. They were easier to fly than Spitfires, allowing new pilots to quickly adjust to battle conditions. Critical issues, such as performance in diving, secure landing and stability of the plane when firing guns were just as important as the Spitfire's sleek profile and innovations. Early in the Battle they were equally powered by the same Merlin engine and armed with identical machine guns. The RAF's 1,715 Hurricanes were responsible for over three-quarters of the Luftwaffe planes taken out of action by Fighter Command.

The Supermarine Spitfire: pride of the RAF

Above: The Supermarine Spitfire, the pride of the RAF and the British nation, was developed in the mid-1930s by Schneider Trophy-winning designer RJ Mitchell. The British government specified that their new generation of fighters should be the fastest possible. Before the addition of armament, the Spitfire with prudent use of its supercharger was very fast and more than a match for the Nazi Bf 109. At a critical phase of the war, Britain was supplied by US aviation fuel that was 100 per cent octane, giving the RAF's fighter planes an edge over the Luftwaffe which used 70 per cent. It was enough to affect the outcome of the Battle.

Opposite: 111 Squadron on patrol; the commander, Sqn. Ldr. J. W. Gillan personally demonstrated the prowess of the Hurricane by flying from Edinburgh to Northolt at an average speed of 408 mph with a journey time of 48 minutes.

Dover's barrage balloons come under fire

Left: In the skies above Dover, two barrage balloons fall to earth in balls of flame. They were attacked by Bf 109s on 1st September, but the balloon crew managed to down one of the Messerschmitts with rifle fire.

Opposite: Two raiding Dornier 17 bombers fly over the Silvertown area of London's Docklands. In this picture, taken from another German aircraft, the famous West Ham greyhound track can be seen near the centre of the photograph

Countering Luftwaffe night bombing missions

Above: A night-fighter crew get a last-minute weather briefing. The Bristol Blenheims that proved so vulnerable over daytime France suited night patrol well: in the night raid on London, 18 June 1940, Blenheims accounted for five German bombers. In July, 600 Squadron, based at RAF Manston, had some of its Mk IFs equipped with AI Mk III radar. With this radar equipment, a Blenheim from the Fighter Interception Unit (FIU) at RAF Ford achieved the first success on the night of 2-3 July 1940, accounting for a Dornier Do 17 bomber. More successes confirmed the Blenheim's invaluable role.

Opposite: Battle of Britain aircraft flew at great height with un-pressurised cabins; from 16,000 feet oxygen was required to maintain consciousness, the cockpit would become very cold and ice could impair mechanics and cloud the plexiglass. To combat the intense cold, the parachute manufacturer Leslie Irvin devised the characteristic airman's jacket from very supple sheepskin, tailored to give maximum warmth whilst allowing freedom to move. The aircrew also wore fleece-lined boots and gloves.

Fabric covered surfaces are shredded in combat

Above This badly shot-up Hurricane of 151 Squadron shows the challenges faced by the RAF in staying operational; losses of pilots and machines often exceeded the rate of supply of replacements. The normal strength of a fighter squadron was 16 aircraft, of which it was assumed that 12 would be operational while four were undergoing repair or maintenance. All too frequently, the operating strength of a squadron could be down to a handful.

Opposite: A glimpse of the spartan interior of the Spitfire cockpit. The steering column or joystick incorporated a red firing button. A gun sight is ranged in the pilot's forward vision. Pilots had to learn how best to fire the Spitfire's machine guns - housed in the wings they affected the aircraft's balance and it was essential that the pilot set up the plane correctly and held the joystick with both hands while firing.

Navigation by dead-reckoning

Opposite: Observers responsible for navigating their night patrol Blenheims plot his course with one of the pilots. Each is using their mechanical flight computer to aid in calculating fuel burn, wind correction, time en route, and other essentials. In the air, the flight computer was used to calculate ground speed as well as wind correction calculations to determine how much the wind was affecting speed and course. Fighter pilots had to do their own navigation, flying by dead reckoning and their version of the manual computer was adapted to fit to their thigh, also containing a flight log.

Right: After returning from a sortie, this pilot is debriefed by an RAF intelligence officer.

'Ginger' Lacey: Britain's most successful Fighter Ace

Above & Opposite: James 'Ginger' Lacey was the RAF ace who, with a tally of 18, brought down more German aircraft than anyone else during the Battle of Britain. On 12th August, the day he was awarded the DFM, he shot up two Ju 87s; on 13th September, he destroyed the Heinkel that bombed Buckingham Palace, a success that brought him a gift of the first parachute made in Australia and a silk scarf embroidered with the names of a hundred girls employed in the factory. In these two photographs the 23-year-old, now Flight Lieutenant, poses for the camera with the scarf and wearing the parachute.

Bader: hero with artificial legs

Opposite: Squadron Leader Douglas Bader of 242 Squadron based at Duxford pictured with his Hurricane in summer 1940. One of the best known pilots of the RAF during World War II, Bader was renowned for his courage and determination. On 14th December 1931, while attempting some low-flying aerobatics at Reading Aero Club's Woodley airfield, his aircraft crashed when a wingtip touched the ground. Bader was rushed to the Royal Berkshire Hospital in Reading, where prominent surgeon Leonard Joyce amputated both his legs. Bader's laconic logbook entry reads: 'Crashed slow-rolling near ground. Bad show.'

Above: Bader, pictured with Pilot Officer W L Knight (r) and Flt Lieut G E Ball (l); they had recently won the DFC while Bader was awarded the DSO. As well as being more experienced than his younger colleagues, it was thought that Bader's missing legs may have given him an advantage in the heavy 'G' manoeuvres: there was no rush of blood away from his head to his legs, as normally experienced by pilots, who had to take care when pulling hard out of dives or making a tight turn - blacking out was a real danger.

Tuck & Johnson: Flying Aces

Above: Squadron Leader Robert Stanford Tuck entered the Battle of Britain with a DFC from his successes over France. He commanded 257 Hurricane Squadron from September and had several lucky escapes until finally shot down over France in 1942 with his tally at 27 kills, having added a DSO to his honours. He escaped German captivity in 1945, fighting alongside the Russians for some time.

Opposite: Pilot Officer James 'Johnnie' Johnson in relaxed mood with his labrador-retriever, Sally, on the wing of his Spitfire. He would become the highest scoring RAF pilot of the war and ended his flying career with the rank of Air Vice-Marshal. Although he flew in the Battle, he was troubled by an old injury and missed much of it when he was hospitalised.

RAF Roll of Honour

Left: This young pilot wears a very non-regulation Mae West decorated with a caricature of the star herself, displaying the pneumatic talent that led to the nickname for the RAF standard issue flotation aid.

Opposite above left: Flt Lieut Patrick 'Paddy' Barthropp DFC began his career with Fighter Command in 602 Squadron based near Chichester, putting him in the thick of conflict.

Opposite above centre: Pilot Officer Richard Hillary joined 603 Squadron in 1940, fresh from Oxford. After shooting down five enemy planes he was downed in September; badly burned, he became one of the best known of pioneering surgeon McIndoe's Guinea Pigs. Before dying in 1943 Hillary wrote an account of being a fighter pilot in 'The Last Enemy.'

Opposite above right: Flying Officer Norman Edgar Ryder served with 41 Squadron, winning his DFC in 1940 but was shot down in September 1941, spending the rest of the war in captivity.

Opposite below left: Squadron Leader DJA Roe gained his command when he was just 23 and wears his DFC ribbon here. By coincidence his father was a sergeant in the same squadron.

Opposite below centre: This unnamed pilot smiles with relief at his safe return from a sortie over the Channel in July 1940.

Opposite below right: Flt Lieut Brian Kingcome was a talented Spitfire pilot attached to 92 Squadron during the Battle. He was awarded his DFC in 1940 and led the squadron on a temporary basis, becoming a Squadron Leader in 1941. Surviving the war he retired in 1954 with the rank of Group Captain and went into business with Paddy Barthropp.

Al Deere - RAF's New Zealand Ace and Battle survivor

Left and opposite: New Zealander Alan 'Al' Deere was one of the RAF's most intrepid pilots and at the end of the Battle was Flight Lieutenant with DFC and bar. His many brushes with death and lucky escapes while shooting down 17 German aircraft, were recorded in his 'Nine Lives' autobiography. He retired in 1977 with the rank of Air Commodore.

'In addition to the skill and gallantry he has shown in leading his flight, and in many instances his squadron, Flight Lieutenant Deere has displayed conspicuous bravery and determination in pressing home his attacks against superior numbers of enemy aircraft, often pursuing them across the Channel in order to shoot them down. As a leader he shows outstanding dash and determination'. - London Gazette quotes his citation on receiving his DFC bar.

Un-named heroes

Opposite: The British nation may have felt under siege during the Battle of Britain and the devastation of the Blitz, but they knew the world was watching the incredible defence being made against Hitler's overwhelming military might. The newspapers idolised the young fighter pilots that challenged the impossible odds, regularly featuring photographs of smiliing young officers. No personal details or reference to which squadron they were attached, holding to the war-time maxim, 'careless talk costs lives'. However the Daily Mail was pleased to record that the pilot bottom left was an American volunteer from Illinois.

Above: Each one of the pilots pictured here had been decorated for his actions in France or the Battle of Britain. They have just returned from a sortie over German-occupied France.

Glamorous heights

Opposite: Brave young pilots and their courageous actions were the lifeblood of newspaper columns when the Battle for France was raging. This pilot was feted for his skill and courage in shooting down a Dornier Do 17 over France.

Right: Squadron Leader Anthony Bartley DFC and bar chalked up eight kills during the Battle and was stationed with 92, 111 and 65 Squadrons. He epitomised the dashing RAF hero and counted Laurence Olivier, Vivien Leigh and Clark Gable among his friends. He is pictured here with his fiancee, the film star Deborah Kerr, whom he married in 1945. His contact with Hollywood led to his becoming a screenwriter and TV producer after the war.

Bader inspires the Canadians of 242 Squadron

Opposite: Four more anonymous pilots who served their country and were singled out to inspire the British public. Inside the oxygen mask of the pilot bottom right can be seen the name RG Marland; he flew with 222 Squadron and died in combat in December 1941.

Above: Douglas Bader led 242 Squadron, formed of Canadian pilots, flying Spitfires. He inspired them to great feats, at one point accounting for 33 downed enemy aircraft during three sorties. Bader and Air Vice-Marshal Trafford Leigh-Mallory, Commander of Fighter Group 12, advocated the 'Big Wing' tactic whereby giant RAF fighter formations gathered to meet the massed Luftwaffe attacks. This doctrine was held even when Air Vice-Marshal Keith Park called for tactical support to guard the battered airfields of 11 Group who bore the worst brunt of German assault. Often, by the time 12 Group had assembled their Big Wing, the German planes had already been turned back or had dropped their bombs and were running for home.

The smiling 'Millionaire Squadron'

Left: Pilots of 601 Squadron pose at the end of the Battle of Britain. Formed originally as an RAF reserve by a cohort of wealthy young men who met at White's Club, this aristocratic unit was also known as the Millionaire Squadron. Included in its ranks were a Guinness heir and Max Aitken, son of the current Lord Beaverbrook, newspaper baron and Minister for Aircraft Production, personally appointed by Winston Churchill. The squadron accounted for more than 100 enemy kills and 10 of its members were awarded the DFC.

The King dons his Air Marshal uniform

Opposite: King George VI and Queen Elizabeth were tireless in their efforts to boost morale among troops and civilians. The King held the rank of Air Marshal of the RAF from 1936 and here greets airmen, himself in service uniform. When Buckingham Palace was bombed, Queen Elizabeth said it was a good thing as they could now look the East End in the face.

Above: This New Zealand pilot quickly downs a cup of tea between sorties at the height of 15th August battles. His squadron leader shares a few words of encouragement. Morale was high amongst the hard-pressed pilots after they learned their losses that day were half those of the Luftwaffe.

Tin-hatted pilots wait on standby

Above: Airfields could be bombed at any time, or a German fighter could appear out of nowhere after flying below radar level to strafe the base. Airfields were equipped with shelters but a direct hit was difficult to survive. Wearing a steel helment during an alert was essential: significant numbers of RAF personnel died or were injured in airfield attacks during the Battle.

Opposite: Confident, smiling RAF pilots look up at the sky, giving a positive message to an anxious nation.

A lucky escape

Left: This fighter pilot, based at Biggin Hill, had a narrow escape on 29th July 1940 when a German bullet grazed his leather flying helmet in a dogfight over Dover. The cockpit had some armour but the plexiglass offered little protection.

Opposite: Pilots of a Coastal Command squadron while away the time waiting for the controller to call. The ubiquitous Nissen hut could be rapidly assembled and, with a stove, offered warmth and shelter from the elements. However it could not withstand aerial attack.

Biggin Hill: a favourite Luftwaffe target

Right: Weary and unshaven airmen of 32 Squadron share a joke at Biggin Hill aerodrome on 31 August 1940. Located in Kent, the airfield was a favourite target for the Luftwaffe. Between August 18th, 1940 and January 7th, 1941, the aerodrome was attacked twelve times. On August 18th, KG 76, a Luftwaffe bomber unit, sent in a high level and low level attack with Dornier Do 17s and Junkers Ju 88s, but the main damage was the cratering of the landing ground. In the second of two attacks on August 30th, a small formation of less than a dozen bombers at low level reduced Biggin Hill to a shambles with 1,000 lb. bombs. Workshops, stores, barracks, WAAF quarters and a hangar were wrecked, and 39 were killed. The next day, a high level attack did further extensive damage, including a direct hit on the Ops block. After the attacks, the airfield was quickly returned to operational status and continued to operate throughout the Battle.

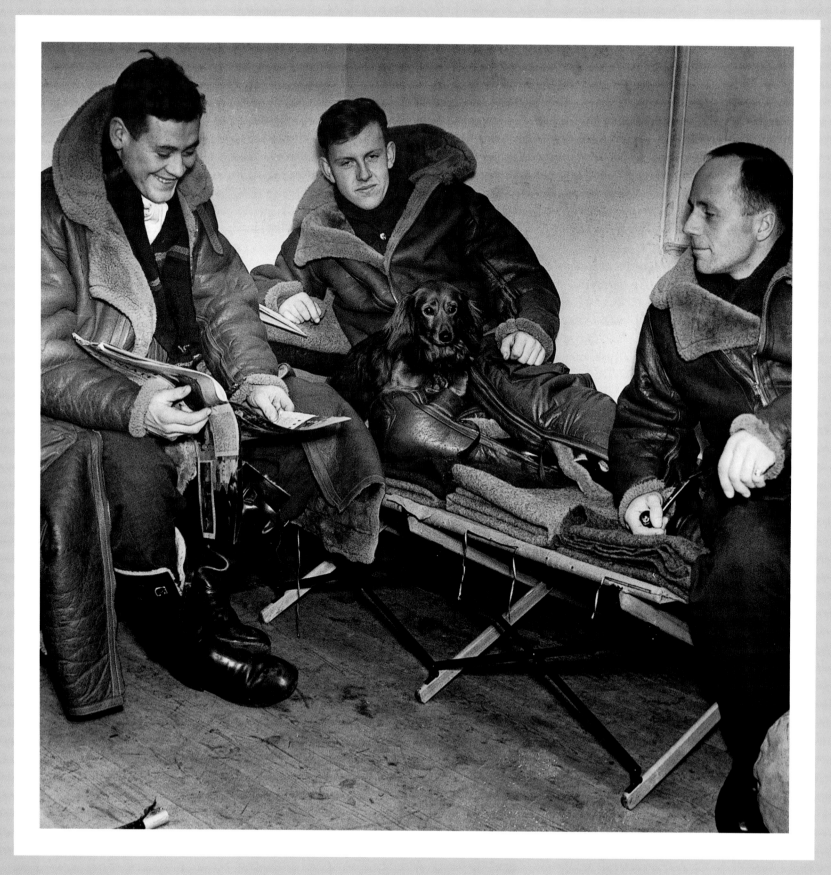

Creature comforts - for some!

Opposite: Most RAF squadrons had a mascot; this well-groomed pooch adds a homely touch to the spartan billet shared by these airmen.

Above: The stove in this airmen's mess provides the warming focal point for the pilots. Their inertia belies the squadron's energy - they had a tally of 60 Luftwaffe kills by the end of 1940.

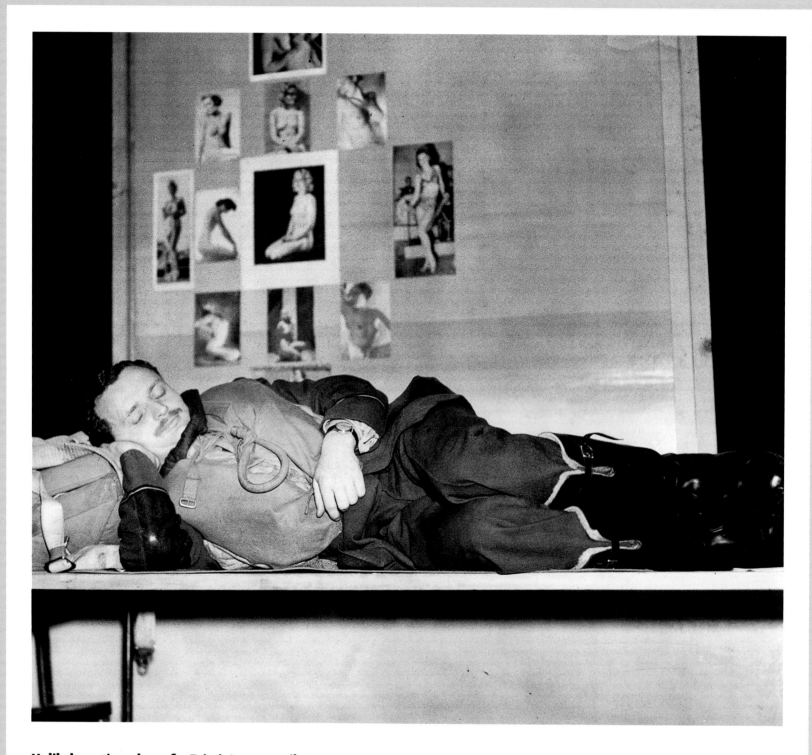

Unlikely resting-places for Britain's weary pilots

Above: An exhausted pilot snatches a quick sleep in between sorties. He lies on a table, without a mattress and uses his parachute as a pillow.

Opposite: Two waiting airmen soak up a bit of sun, snoozing on the bare boards outside their station.

Lining up for the kill

Above: These pilots seem to be taking bar skittles just as seriously as their protection of the skies over Britain.

Opposite: Pilots of the National Air Communications pool eat supper at their West Country mess. The main airlines counted on ex-service pilots as employees; many civilian pilots were still RAF reserve and pilots that normally would have retired were being retained for the war effort. National Air Communications was created to manage the supply of pilots for civil aviation and gave rise to the Air Transport Authority which provided non-combatant flyers to ferry planes around the country - especially delivery of new aircraft. Many women became experienced pilots in the ATA.

Planning the next move...

Opposite and above: Airmen entertain themselves with a mixture of bar games, from shove ha'penny and darts to chess. Such entertainment might be spartan by today's standards but was the norm in a society where people occupied themselves without TV. Radio was a standard provision, however, and a single Home Service broadcast in Britain until the Forces Programme began broadcasting in January 1940. The focus here was on entertaining the troops and boosting military and civilian morale. This gave rise to music programmes like *Works Wonders*, that eventually became '*Workers Playtime*' - a six-week series that lasted 23 years.

Saluting greatness

Above: King George VI receives an enthusiastic salute from the men of this fighter squadron where he was awarding military medals. To be decorated by the King in person was regarded as the ultimate honour.

Opposite: Pilot Officer William 'Billy' Fiske is laid to rest in Boxgrove, Surrex. One of a handful of American volunteer pilots, Fiske was one of the first to die in the Battle after being shot down on 16th August 1940. He joined 601 Squadron where, being from a wealthy family and married to a countess, he was at home with friends and peers in the Millionaire Squadron. Fiske was a colourful character and an Olympic gold medallist.

Production targets soar

Above: Over 3,000 Miles Master trainer aircraft were built after it came into service just before the war. The two-seater monoplane was strong, manoeuvrable and fast - an ideal introduction for future Hurricane and Spitfire pilots. All aircraft were built in one factory next to the airfield, near Reading, where Douglas Bader had the crash that cost him his legs.

Opposite: By the outbreak of war, 18 squadrons had been equipped with nearly 500 Hurricanes but this was well behind the Air Ministry target, whose latest demand took Hawker's order book to 3,500 planes. Main production was divided between Hawker's works and the Gloster factory in the west of England; between them the initial order was completed by the Battle, however production had to remain high to replace lost aircraft - 200 of them in the short Battle for France. Their simple construction made for fast production.

New tactical aircraft for Bomber Command

Right: The limitations of the Bristol Blenheim led to the development of the Beaufort, which entered service with a Coastal Command squadron in 1940. Just over 2,000 were built with the bulk of production at Blackburn's Yorkshire works. The light bomber was intended to carry torpedoes to be used against the German navy and in aerial mine-laying as well as short-range. From July 1940 to the end of the year, Bomber Command lost nearly 330 aircraft and over 1,400 aircrew killed, missing or PoW.

Home of the Spitfire

Right: Supermarine's first production line of the Spitfire at its Woolston plant looks impressive but was tiny in comparison with Britain's need to re-arm. The Air Ministry's order for the first 310 was delayed and proved expensive at £9,500 per machine. To boost production, a model factory was built at Castle Bromwich but it was painfully slow in coming online. When Lord Beaverbrook was appointed Minister for Aircraft Production he cut through the red tape that beset government institutions: appointing experienced managers from Vickers-Armstrong to control the new Spitfire factory was just one of the actions taken by Beaverbrook to double production in 1940. In the first four months of 1940, 2,729 aircraft were produced, 638 of them fighters; in the following four months May to August, 4,578 planes were built - 1,875 fighters. The new rate of production was more than double that of Germany's fighter production. When production of the Spitfire ended in 1945, more than 12,000 had been built.

Fund-raising delivers presentation Spitfires

Opposite: The symbol of the Spitfire and the bravery of its pilots gained the backing of the entire nation; Beaverbrook's Spitfire Fund led to organisations of all sizes raising money to 'buy' Spitfires, which entered service with appropriate names. Here 19-year-old Nora Margaret Fish hands over a Spitfire named 'Counter Attack' on behalf of the NAAFI canteen workers who raised the money in October 1940. The Kennel Club was responsible for 'The Dog Fighter' and Marks & Spencer, 'The Marksman'.

Above: This shot-down Messerschmitt Bf 109 went on display to raise money for the Croydon Spitfire Fund; a high proportion of the estimated 1,500 'Presentation Spitfires' were funded in this way. Those who couldn't afford money donated their pots and pans as raw materials for manufacturing.

Keeping the shipping lanes open

Opposite: At the outbreak of war, Britain was still very much a maritime nation; as an island it was dependent on the merchant navy for trade and transport of bulk goods. Furthermore the Royal Navy was the Senior Service of Britain's military might and an industry in itself. Germany opened its hostiities with aerial and submarine attacks on Britain's shipping; immediately, defensive tactics had to be put in place in British waters. Here a convoy sails along the east coast.

Above: The North Sea fishing fleet was important to British food resources and its vessels increasingly came under attack in the early months of 1940. This picture records an ironic reversal when local fishermen carry officers of the RAF's fishery protection (the so-called 'Kipper Patrol') ashore after a ride in a lifeboat.

Essential convoys ply the English Channel

Above: The wide expanses of the Atlantic were impossible for the Royal Navy to patrol effectively against submarines. All shipping sailed in convoy with naval escort and aerial protection from Coastal Command wherever possible.

Opposite: HMS *Green Fly* was a trawler converted to naval use as an escort vessel and lookout for German E boats; its armament was one four-inch gun and two machine guns housed in sponsons either side of the bridge. Its rudimentary anti-submarine equipment would have been little use against hunting pairs of submarines. In this dramatic photograph, shells burst near the convoy as it sails along the Channel; they have been fired from long-range German guns located on the French coast.

Attacks from aircraft and shore-based artillery

Opposite above: In summer 1940, a convoy is attacked by German aircraft while passing through the Straits of Dover; smoke and spray from the bomb that has missed its target shoot high in the air.

Opposite: Viewed from the cliffs of Dover, this photograph captures another attack on a British convoy by the long-range guns on the French coast.

German artillery in France get dangerously close

Above: Just outside the Dover harbour fortifications, a German shell narrowly misses this ship. Under the right conditions the long-range guns on the French coast could land shells on the port and town of Dover.

Opposite: The boat in the foreground ferries barrage balloons for delivery to an outbound convoy. While close to shore in busy estuary shipping lanes, the balloons gave cover from dive bombers and were an important part of shipping protection.

Protecting the skies around Britain's coast

Opposite: The calm waters of Dover's large harbour erupt with exploding bombs while an anti-aircraft barrage fills the sky with deadly dark puffs causing enemy fighters to take evasive action.

Above: The Royal Naval Patrol Service was part of the Navy's Auxiliary Fleet and played a major role during the war. Recruited from the ranks of fishermen and civilian sailors, the Service escorted convoys around Britain, the Atlantic and the Russian Sea; they also manned minesweepers. On this training vessel, the crew, former fishermen, carry out anti-aircraft drill.

Royal Navy called south to meet the threat of invasion

Opposite: Warships of the Royal Navy plough through choppy seas, their guns at the ready. In July 1940, Allied shipping losses in British waters peaked at 67 vessels sunk, nearly 200,000 combined tonnage. The great ships of the Royal Navy were called south from Scapa Flow in anticipation of the imminent German invasion.

Left: Crew of the Fleet Air Arm go over charts in their mess. The Royal Navy had its own aircraft at the beginning of the century but merged with the Royal Flying Corps to form the RAF in 1918. The Navy continued to fly ship-based aircraft as tactical weapons but the great changes in warfare slowly forced the imperial powers to recognise the importance of air power and the Fleet Air Arm was formed under admiralty control in 1939. By the end of the War, aircraft carriers became the capital ships in the navies of the world and the Fleet Air Arm operated nearly 4,000 aircraft from 59 carriers.

Naval reserve officers get the latest briefing

Above: In mid December 1940, officers of the Royal Naval Volunteer Reserve (RNVR) receive instruction about enemy aircraft attacks. The Reserve corps comprised highly qualified civilian seamen who held rank equivalent to opposite numbers in the full-time service and could be deployed as needed. Not only did they provide officers for naval duties, but RNVR also provided pilot officers for similar deployment in the Fleet Air Arm.

Opposite: Spitfire pilots in their Scottish base await the controller's call to scramble in April 1941.

Spitfires given more powerful armament

Opposite: The latest Spitfire, equipped with two wing-mounted 20mm cannon, practises aerial tactics on this RAF trainer during exercises. The veteran pilots and Fighter Command reckoned that a pilot needed a year of flying to be sufficiently trained to meet the Luftwaffe challenge. During the Battle, novices were filling the ranks of their lost and wounded seniors, leading to increased casualties.

Opposite: A black pall of smoke rises from the English countryside marking the location of a downed Messerschmitt. Sent as escorts with the waves of bombers, the German fighters had sufficient fuel for about 10 minutes flying over London, before being forced to return to base.

A change in the tide: A new German tactic

Opposite: In October 1940, Germany stood down its Operation Sealion invasion forces and what remained of the barges that hadn't been sunk by British bombing were dispersed. The Battle of Britain, Hitler's attempt to gain mastery of the British skies might have failed but the Blitz continued to be a potent and almost crushing strategy. However, the RAF, freed from the pressure of massed daytime raids and the need to engage hundreds of Luftwaffe fighters could now move onto the offensive and began regular sweeps over occupied France, harrassing German troops and destroying their defensive positions.

Above: The Spitfire came through the Battle of Britain with flying colours, proving itself not just to be a sleek, high-speed fighter, but an efficient killing machine, thanks to continuing improvements: finally its carburettor was adapted to enable a dive as steep as the Bf 109 and the limited machine guns were beefed up with wing-mounted cannon. Further developments were made to the Rolls-Royce Merlin engine and improved propellers stepped up the plane's performance. The variant shown here sports the new cannon with a cowling covering adaptations for deployment in north Africa's Western Desert.

The Luftwaffe shifts to night bombing: the Blitz begins

Above: Hurricanes patrol the skies. RDF provided efficient screening for the massed Luftwaffe attacks of the Battle of Britain but German planes learned to fly under the radar and the RAF daylight patrols were the only sure way to intercept attacking and reconnaissance aircraft.

Opposite: Daylight attacks by the Luftwaffe more or less ended on 29th October 1940 but were substituted with devastating night raids. The Hurricane received further adaptations to make it effective by day and by night as an interceptor. As can be seen in this formation of 87 Squadron, parading its brand-new Mark IIC aircraft donated by the people of the United Provinces of India, the colour scheme of the aircraft has been darkened considerably while its armament now boasts four wing-mounted 20mm cannon.

US high-octane fuel gives British fighters an advantage

Above: Three Hurricanes refuel. Each of these aircraft burned the entire year's petrol ration for a private motorist in two hours of flying. All the RAF's high-octane fuel had to travel by convoy across the Atlantic and its cost was not in money but in human lives and sunk ships. The USA was helpful to a point, but was reticent at once more being drawn into a European conflict. This would change with the Japanese attack on the US fleet in Pearl Harbor in December 1941.

Opposite: The latest version of the Spitfire - Mk Vb of 92 Squadron shows off its new features in early summer of 1941. Able to achieve speeds approaching 400mph, it would achieve superiority over current German planes until the arrival of the Focke-Wulf 190. The aircraft pictured was used personally by the RAF ace, Alan Wright.

'We shall never stop, never weary and never give in'

Opposite: Winston Churchill receives a rapturous welcome in Sheffield as people crowd his open car to greet him. The nation was in no doubt that Churchill's indomitable leadership brought them through the Battle of Britain and that his objective was unchanged from his first speech to Parliament as Prime Minister: total victory over the Nazi regime, 'Victory at all costs'.

Above: Assembled to take their place at Winston Churchill's funeral in 1965, these surviving veterans of the Battle of Britain still served in the RAF and all held the rank of Group Captain except for Alan Deere seventh from left who was Air Commodore. These were indeed 'The Few'.

Spitfire supremacy

Opposite: 611 Squadron flies out with its spanking new Spitfire Mk IXs produced to meet the challenge of the FW 190 in December 1942. A larger engine and four-blade propeller were just two of the improvements that boosted performance.

Right: The Mark XII version of the Spitfire took to the air in April 1942, equipped with the much more powerful Griffon engine and a strengthened airframe to take advantage of the extra horsepower. Only 100 went into production as a speed advantage at lower altitudes compromised performance at high altitudes. In effect it was a prototype for the much more successful Mk XIV that entered service in January 1943, with dramatic improvements to its climb rate and top speed.

Symbolic moment

Opposite: With the Battle of Britain proving that the German war machine was not invincible, British confidence mustered to see the nation through the dark days of the Blitz. From then on the clock was ticking, especially after the US joined the war; it was now a matter of time before a hard-fought series of campaigns would release Europe from Nazi domination. In a symbolic moment, Britain's Field Marshal Bernard Montgomery is welcomed to Copenhagen by RAF ace Johnnie Johnson in May 1945.

Above: World War II has an endless list of heroes. Few showed greater determination and survival ability than Squadron Leader Douglas Bader. That a man without legs should fly fighter aircraft in a leadership role was testimony enough but then to survive while so many others died; to be shot down and imprisoned in the depths of Germany but then to ceaselessly resist, making many escape attempts set this man apart, marking him as a hero. Finally released from the notorious prison camp Colditz, he made his way to Paris and attempted to requisition a Sptifire so he could return to battle for the final phase of the war.

Winston Churchill caught in a quiet moment. His ironic look, cigar in hand and his iconic black felt Bowker hat and stick laid on the table make him seem very human. Yet if the RAF were 'the Few' he was 'the One'.

Acknowledgements

The photographs in this book are from the archives of the Daily Mail.

Particular thanks to Alan Pinnock